WALKING ON FROGS

Also by John Cassidy

The Dancing Man (Poet's Yearbook, 1977)
An Attitude of Mind (Hutchinson, 1978)
Changes of Light (Bloodaxe Books, 1979)
The Fountain (Bloodaxe Books, 1979)
Night Cries (Bloodaxe Books, 1982)

JOHN CASSIDY

Walking
on
Frogs

BLOODAXE BOOKS

ISBN: 1 85224 089 X

First published 1989 by
Bloodaxe Books Ltd,
P.O. Box 1SN,
Newcastle upon Tyne NE99 1SN

Bloodaxe Books Ltd acknowledges
the financial assistance of Northern Arts.

Typesetting by EMS Phototypesetting, Berwick upon Tweed.

Printed in Great Britain by
Bell & Bain Limited, Glasgow, Scotland.

For my family

Acknowledgements

Acknowledgements are due to the editors of the following publications in which some of these poems first appeared: *Acumen, Critical Quarterly, The Honest Ulsterman, Outposts, Poetry Review, Poetry Voice, Poetry with an Edge* (Bloodaxe Books, 1988), *Smoke, Stand* and *051*. 'Crossings', 'Boulder City', 'The Wasp Trap' and 'Well-Heads' were broadcast on *Poetry Now* (BBC Radio 3); 'Crossings' was also broadcast on *Poems from Abroad* (BBC Radio 4).

Contents

I. COAST TO COAST

FRAGMENTS
OF AMERICA

New York Harbour

They cut into the light,
the hard edges of things;
buildings like upended streets
take up a share of the sky
with this one razored gull
careering over the Hudson.
He crosses the wakes of ferries,
slipping occasionally down the air
letting his legs dangle, bill
open and expectant,
to hoick something unnoticeable
out of the water and lift away
with his valued minimal loot.
His eye is enviable.
From all that wash and swell,
that space, he takes what he needs
then swings his white away
across that extravagantly famous
landfall. I like the way of it.
I slip into his style.

Manhattan

The schist is what started it.
Just about the hardest rock
Anywhere on the continent

And what better to hold up
Blocks like these? Nothing,
Nowhere, could rival it.

Never till then had anyone
Dared upward so many storeys.
Now you can spot them, these first

Thirty-odd floor amazements,
Dainty as old ladies under
The engineered mountain walls alongside.

Broadway, they say,
That island-long diagonal,
Was an Indian hunting trail.

Timescapes here are believable.
The Chrysler building in its thirties dress
Is quaint as thatched cottages back home.

Farm in Pennsylvania

Near the flat of the valley
where the slope bottoms out,
the farm buildings, small house
and big barn, hold onto their space.

Above, the woods have the look
of something pushed back, held,
waiting to drop down and overwhelm
the skylit clearings. Up there
the deer will be watching,
slithering through the birches.

The fields in cultivation stay
near to home, asway with a drift
of cattle, or nodding with corn.
Alongside the house, close,
lie the strict vegetable rows,
and a twisted orchard struggles
behind the barn.
                    Over a wall
is a smaller field with the one certain
harvest, perhaps a dozen grey-white
headstones, where the graves are.

At a House of Robert Frost

In Dearborn at the Henry Ford Museum
they've built a village humouring the old
America, shipping the houses here
from everywhere across the continent.

Clean lettering on a painted board
sets out that Robert Frost
had this pine home way back
and way up North of Boston.

The tourist buggies rubber-wheel along
behind calm horses; beds of herbs
perplex the air in the noon sun.
The grass is laundered, the trees tamed.

This couldn't be New Hampshire,
nor one of the five farms in Vermont.
The woods are empty of promises,
no one swings on the birches. Still,

put your hand here. I'd guess the stoop
vibrates, right where his boots
clumped down in the pale daybreak,
when he went out to clean the pasture spring.

Walking in Chicago

You've got to lift your chin
  Quite some way
To see where the tops of the buildings
  Rise to, shining against the clouds.

Up there the late sun
  Flatters their glass and metal.
Shaded below
  The traffic and the sidewalks
Crawl in a duller heat,
  Though the street walls have a polish
To brighten the eyes' track up to where the sun strikes.

Then the lakefront
  Swinging round
Opens suddenly in an infinity
  Of sky and scudding water.
Michigan is a blur of sails.

Along there the grassland throws up trees,
  Tennis courts, flower-beds, ball games
Before a frieze of immense towers
  Like rockets at lift-off
Spiking the prairie sky.

The clouds are rolling evenly from the east
  And the wind
Presses itself against everything,
  Parkland, water, the sails
As they negotiate their little passages,
  The towers uttering their incredible ambitions
To the plains, the city that shoulders
  Even the sun out of its way
And lives in the shadowed alleys
  Caged and uncontainable.

Thunder in Missouri

All night a drum-roll of thunder
   had parallelled sleep.
Even at daybreak green swathes
   of light flickered incessantly
against the sky and into our dull room.

Headlamps along the highway
   beamed into walls of rainfall
and across the Missouri river
   billows of smoky downpour
wandered away over Iowa.

It was a day like other days,
   a Tuesday morning and work
spreading its routines and rumbling on:
   every driver behind the dark
holes the wipers evenly made

in the windshield's skin of wet
   was stuck there in his Tuesday
morning seat and going all out
   wherever Tuesday took him.
The spray was yards high for miles.

The sky was bigger than ever
   going on over all horizons
beyond the penetration of the eye;
   its thumping mallet blows
flattening the whole land out

making everything metal-coloured
   river road buildings grass
and the leaning-over trees:
   the brave shines of the chains of traffic
a ridiculous minute defiance.

New Orleans

The moon hangs like the last cantaloupe
on the market, in its net of cloud.
Even at this small hour there will be some
slung yet over quiet traders down
that end of town.
               Music
splutters out of the bars and falls
into the streets, where tangles of people
mooch and spread, their faces agleam
like the pottery carnival masks
hilarious in the stores; they are glazed
it seems armoured in joy.
                   Out further,
in the wide reaches of darkness,
police-cars howl like sad cats
and forage among shadows.
There is a blood-scent on the grid.
No night can be different.
                 Later,
the moon slips from its net
and lifts, brightens into a white
dominance, and pulls what could be
hope, what feels like hope, necessary
neutral illumination,
along the glittering and enormous river.

Oklahoma City

Outside the Capitol
Is the cowboy statue under the tree,
With small shades dancing
On the flanks of the once wild
Pony gripped between his thighs.

Over the road in open sun
The derrick atop the oil-well
Is a pyramid of glitter.
It will have you frowning,
Lowering your eyes.

The cool museum's statue
The End of the Trail
Is white and gigantic. The ghost
Indian slumps astraddle,
The horse is collapsing like a snowbank.
In the high-ceilinged room
You can almost hear
Their harsh, last breathings.

Noon in Santa Fe

High-nosed trucks
   with snorting upright pipes
get between us and the Indians.
   They sit beyond the traffic
with their spread jewellery, their bread
   big as pillows, their prune-pie,
shaded under the colonnade.

And about the plaza
   pale, splay-brimmed hats
move pools of shadow slowly
   from awning to awning
round the fawn adobe buildings,
   banks, offices, hotels,
and girls are rollerskating
   silently, with elastic limbs
and lifting, sun-bleached hair.

Close, hard, knife-edged,
   the mountains jag into the sky,
where a few blinding clouds, white
   as imagination, balance
and stretch. It is as if
   something is waiting, some
utterly undomestic possibility
   hangs in the blue.
The air shimmers over the trucks'
   shaking engines.
The heat is volcanic.

Store

The health inspector's car
   which she parked at the store
has a Navajo Nation crest on the door.

Some of her possible charges
   are unloading their trolleys
onto the boards of their flatback Chevvies.

I buy some film. The girl
   smiles a Navajo smile at the till.
Round me mutter the click and moil

of a difficult tongue, flinty,
   brittle in the big silence of empty
scrubland, flight-feather-quick flicking into

the clutter of coke-tins and candles.
   Two girls, whose tar-river hair reaches
the backs of their jeans, come out with ices.

They lick keenly; their tongues grow numb;
   Their talk is of videos; their fingers drum
on the hood; they wait for their slow parents to come.

The Landscape Speaks, Near Flagstaff

Snow on the crowns of mountains
Operates till July,
Durable even under that indigo sky.

Disappointingly the yuccas
Open themselves in flowers
During the season of encouraging showers

Only, and that's in spring.
From summer through the fall
There'll be no noticeable bloom at all

Though trees, except the firs,
Will entertain in dress
Of painful, dying vividness.

I always work to schedule,
Turning with the earth.
The flora and fauna know what that's worth.

And this, given the scale,
Should be enough. From snow
To furnace-dust, unsubtle I know,

But this is blatant country,
No hints, no ambiguities, no lies.
I give you what you call realities.

Dry River Bed, Arizona

Water spills a few threads over
Those wide, warm rocks,
Buries itself in the gravel
Or slips into cracks
    As if asking for dark

Like the gophers that quiver
Their muzzles in quick
Interrogation out of their clever
Network of tunnels, then double back
    Sinuously into the dark,

So that everything moving
Seems to be moving inward,
Sliding a glance then diving
Out of the air's vacuous regard,
    Choosing again the dark.

So the vital must take cover,
Deeply away from the sun
And the other raptors that hover
And swing in ferocious light, down
    To investigate the dark

And its multiple promises, never
Final in all its windings, nor
Stark, nor positive. The dead river
World, so absolute, so clear,
    Should recommend the dark.

Boulder City

In late afternoon the sun
has begun its drop.
There are shadows now, precise
as black paint. Not even
a flurry of dust moves
not even a hint of cirrus.
The thermometer stands
at a hundred and, say,
thirteen.
      Easterners settle here
out of the river fogs
and the greening rain.
Their sprawled houses are silent
beside the blue geometry
of their deserted pools.
That water now must be
fit to simmer a chicken.
Indoors these pioneers lie low
in the blast of the air-conditioning.
Should they step from home the sun
will lean on their skulls like a ton of fire.

Sea Lions off Monterey

Half a mile into the Pacific
a rock like the back of a sea-beast
humps itself out; the swell sounds
hollowly as it bumps the sides even
in slack water, the sides the only bits
visible under the sea lions
crowding the top, still, mostly,
as clusters of mussels.
                              On shore
round the coin-op telescope
the children bounce and wrangle,
and the cars slide down to the shore
and slide away again. An encounter
on the edge of things, the sea's curled
lip, the end of a continent,
the abounding other, leaving
nothing to be said.
                              The still,
head-up animals stare
indifferently out of the ocean.

Waiting for the Cable Car

The banjo, the harmonica,
somewhere by the head of the line
are enjoying themselves.
Two hundred people are listening
or partly listening. That instrument,
says the engineer from New Jersey,
is the only authentic American
musical invention, the banjo.
Does he apologise or boast?
Its pluck and babble float about,
sway the crowd, make all those feet
restless; we talk in rhythm till
the car clangs in, and the music men
push out their hats, and all
San Francisco has suddenly gone
quiet, dull, ordinary, musicless.

II WALKING ON FROGS

Equipoise

We know that spreading branches
Are balanced underground;
Leaves raft in the wind
On noisy summer nights
While a mute net of roots
Strains with the earth it clutches.

The dizzy office tower
Stirs in a heavy wind.
From far above the ground
We see the landscape move
Perceptibly, and prove
The base, the grip, the power.

While daring into chance
The energies will ask
Congruity. The risk
Must match the hidden
Anchoring; ambition
Bites both ways at once.

But earth is rougher far
Than air, and tricky ground
More treacherous than wind.
The dark reach into soil
Will not make roots prevail
Nor safety certain, ever.

Tensions

During a long winter
Blasts of wind across the flat lands
Tackled a few big trees, and clipped
Innumerable chimney-pots.
Cascades of slates battered the pavements
And windows splashed into bedrooms
Letting the sleet in an hour before dawn.

None of this could be shrugged off.
The bass roaring in the woods,
The high whining filling the wires
Sang wickedly together.
Hunched into collars we pushed outdoors
At the edge of light, sensing
A focused malevolence, ourselves

Picked out as targets for all this.
Something was after us; it was
Up there at roof level, throwing
Loose bits down, it was behind
The protesting tree, tearing its roots
Out ready, it was angling
The world into hostility: it would

Get us before the sun made light
Of it all and the pressure changed
And the winds died and we walked
Belittled in a world not at all
Concentrating on us any more and the sky
Cleared for the wheeling of careless birds
And the routine slack circles of the clock.

One Long Blue Note

One long blue note
moans from the gape of a saxophone
to the skitter and thud skitter
and thud of the drum.

That plangency
holds and withholds all its promisings
clear and away from the timebound
rhythmic drive below.

Something floats there
papery and crisp as currency
riding the moment, generous
and extravagant

and absolving;
but it hungers too for the bristle
of tricky drumbeats patterning
the earth's gravity.

The measuring
tread restricts and decorates the winged
adventuring. Which lives in stress
alone, in stress, stress.

The Flaw

Greenery dresses the lake
Offering reeds to the shallows;
Ruinous mud-spits
Finger out from the shore.

Week by week the broad
Water shrinks from the banks
And the palmate feet of coot
Leave longer tracks.

A secret fissure is leaking
The whole lake away,
A treachery nobody knows of
But the deepest of the sluggish tench.

If this goes on those slow
Bronze fish will find themselves
Desperately flattening down
Into the last wet inches.

Their small gapes will round
As if howling out hurt
And accusation at the thin
Hidden wound killing all of them.

It will be no use. Something has struck
Way beneath where any healing
Can possibly reach. Their trust
And ours will shrivel and then choke.

Precaution

Smile at everyone as if
Most of them are moderately
Benign.
      Move into crowds
On quiet feet. Keep your eyes
Mobile, your ears alert.

Know that there is always one
Silent and behind you, who
Stands where you are never
Looking, in some alcove of your life
And, choosing a runnel in the ribs,
Slides in the knife.

Nocturne

Dismal as a toad's domed eye, a cloud
Across the sundown's duck-egg blank
Yellows at the edges; its mass
Leans on itself, clambers, swells
Over itself, layering up and up.
Sleep threatens like a suffocation.

Think of freedoms: feel wind,
Smell bracken, listen to leaves.
Lie under rattling aspens
Or a clumped oak. But there,
Stuck close to the trunk,
An undiagnosed lump, secret

From the light, hugs itself ready,
Ready to lift open the stare
Of a killing eye, and clack
Rehearsing billhook mandibles
For the inevitable sweet sunfall.
It will launch out moth-like, shrieking.

Minotaur

It is there in the dark
a blacker piece of the black
I can see nothing no silhouette
of horns no nostril no roll of eye-white

I can hear the shift of weight
the heavy rhythms of breath
I fancy the dull beat of a pulse
I can hear the malevolence

in the net of passages
I have contrived for it
secure as a lattice of thick bars
secure as a pit
the deeper shadow lurks and stirs

youth is crunched there it swallows
maidens and I Daedalus
of my craftsmanship have made
its home, deep, central, as
even its begetting I engineered

my skill it lives in, my life is equal
to it, should it appear
the shape would be unrecognisable
as monstrous being too familiar

Scenario for a Dream

You are leading the raid.
Among the neglected trees
Surrounding the target house
Your colleagues are posted, with dogs.
Car tracks scar the shallow mud
On the path to the path to the door
Which opens without a key. You
Climb the stairs, quietly, seeing
The door at the top that you know is
The door.
        Movement behind it
Stops your climb. You listen,
Thumb on the safety-catch. And shout.

Come out with your hands in the air,
Slowly, one at a time.

Now. Now you will know, really
Know. And you simultaneously
Know that the gun is defective, probably
Jammed, perhaps, paralysingly,
A piece of wood.
The squad in the shrubs was never
There. You shout for the dogs
And there comes no galloping bark.
· There is only you.
Always there has only been you.

The one to come out of the door
The one you have come here for
The one who will walk out alone
The one who has turned you to stone
Is going to be, you know it, he too
Is going to be
You.

The door handle dips and the gap
Appears, widens and widens.

33

B

Tactic

I am walking the wall
　　in a rough March.
From the far side of it

come volleys of hostile
　　sleet and the snatch
of an explosive gust

wrong-footing me every
　　yard. On my side
the cultured green pasture

shines in the wet. Over
　　the wall's blunt blade
the drab long-haired moor-grass

is frantic: barbarous
　　territory
ululating and lost.

I turn my stinging face
　　defensively
downwind, prizing the neat

civil fields, the comfort
　　of suave acres,
the tarmac road to town.

The wall sighs but does not
　　shift; its fissures
whistle an unbroken

elegy signalling
　　the humped, final
stand of its gritstone and

desperation. The flung
　　sky, air, ground, all
agitated beyond

containment, are certain
　　to pour over,
riot and occupy

and transform. Better, then,
　　to box clever,
master a new patois,

stay out in the open,
　　rapid mover,
disguising a despair.

On the Bridge

The water is a slate bed
with raw quarry marks
rippling it, solid
flat and fast flowing.
From here you can feel the hard
breaking of anything
dropping onto it,
the bony crack before the splash.

How far up would the ragged
subsiding edge of water
climb? Would the bottom strut
feel any spray?
How long would a body float?
Could a mile downstream
be where it is finally clawed
to shore? Is this what he wonders?

Chin on the balustrade
too high for elbows, what is he
looking at? The sick sky's lid
on his world, the down-river
line of rooftops, or the dead
back of his eyelids, closed,
blacking it all out?
The wind plucks at his face.

If the noticeable world
sags like a wet fleece,
impenetrable, cold,
inwardly he is rich in pigments,
theatrically lit.
Instead of the drama of the long
drop, a solo sprawled
finale, he can retract

spitefully into the prepared
space under the skull,
thick with images and ruled
by no force he has allegiance to,
not even circumstance. Foiled
by the dull impossibilities, he slips
deftly back inside his head,
to make it all happen there.

Kafka's Funeral

It should have been raining lead
   that Prague June.
   More probably, though, the sun shone
   instead. The sky would have been
very uninterested.

It was not a large gathering
   bunched at the graveside, silent.
   Max Brod, humped and intent,
   gave the one speech, a lament,
a claim, an honouring.

The box was ready to go, Kafka
   becoming at last the mole
   he always felt he was, to steal
   along the winding tunnels
of his secret castle,

or to burrow as he used to, furled
   under his sick man's bedclothes, still
   and safe, and see himself sail
   his books away adventuring into the real
and difficult world.

The distraction when it came
   came from that world, a woman, dark,
   twentyish, who broke
   decorum, and in the shock
of a moment's numb

surprise, flung hair,
   arms, body and passionate wailing
   in a wild restraining
   struggle over the gaping
trench. Kafka's father

turned his wide back.
    Someone or other helped her, bent
    to her trembling shoulders, lent
    her a kind of calm, and the spent
tears dried on her cheek.

The itch of them she would wince
    away from even when her small name slid
    from sight, and her rich hair paled,
    and the man that she thought she held
hers only was everyone's.

These two had fused and faded. Soon
    his dark books would glow in a space
    whirling at some indefinite distance
    from that agonised, now more or less
irrelevant, Prague afternoon.

Call-box, Midnight

Darkness is more than absence
  of light. Trees in the suburb
    hug themselves in fog and slide

beads down their grooved bark.
  The telephone box beams like a Christmas
    candle; inside, your tears

glitter and scatter tinselly
  over your collar. The message
    is muffled, coughed out, cut short

as I pass. The receiver tings
  wittily as the door groans open
    to let you out. Your footsteps

knock and knock fadingly away.
  Your black dress is swallowed by dark,
    by time, by catastrophe.

You go off walking, walking
  somewhere, whatever it was,
    whoever you are.

Bracelet

That touching metal
   deceives; its cool smooth
      skin polishes skin

and burnishes itself.
   It takes up warmth
      and retains it briefly

thus seeming to give.
   Its innocent integument
      covers a wiry heart.

It plays with fugitive light
   catching whatever it can
      to dispense as its own;

starlight on frost, you could say,
   or sun on a railway line,
      would not outstare it.

It has its dangers, then,
   for you who wear it;
      such images might be,

when all is said, too near
   whatever truth vibrates
      under those invisible follicles.

A Photograph of Your Friends

One of your friends is in silver,
   the other in black: an obvious
pair, slumped on a padded settle;
   their legs shine without fuss,
their emptied glasses teeter,
   they are contemptuous of us.

Silver's intent on the lens,
   Black is intent on her.
Silver smiles firmly as if
   the lens is her bedroom mirror
and her teeth secret omens.
   Black is lunging to splutter

a kiss on the turning jaw
   and test her palm along
a silver thigh. For her
   the camera, like everything
outside herself, is a minor flaw
   in the world, a mild aberration.

There the disco sound encloses
   and invades with its big feel.
Your friends, you claim, are vibrant,
   raw, you have got to say, real;
this fixes one of their phases.
   Their eyes are flat and unexcitable.

They're much like you, you say,
   hoping I'll think you mistaken;
or partly so, for a part
   of you wants to be partly taken
as living inside your own law,
   sublimely silver, or black and stricken.

Graveyard with Orange-Tree

One big orange-tree lifts from the graveyard.
When an almost undetectable stir
of air moves the leaves, clear
richly coloured fruit accept the sun.
There is a hanging quiet, unimpaired
by the seep and hiss of water from thin
galvanised pipes coming out of the stone.

On the graves are the framed photographs of
the recently dead. Their faces
are sombre, as if preparing for this.
The clean glass glints over them.
From beyond history the beehive graves
on the tall hillside opposite affirm
their white surviving requiem.

The small church here stares back at them.
It is round, solid, fiercely white as they,
and holds its ground as blankly.
Over the low walls grape bunches
like the hands of marauders swarm
and hook themselves in place.
The afternoon light remains at ease.

These allegiances to the dead
impose their reassurance.
The orange-tree swings an exuberance
of sunlit fruit over roots in the soil
of graves, flowered and tended:
all this pattern of logics, exact and small,
thoughts stretched over the unthinkable.

At an Outdoor Café

The sun flattens your hair
hot along your scalp.
Touch it and you scorch,
fingers and scalp both,
and the hair bids to kindle
tindery, brittle, sweatless.

Mine is like that, too.
I refuse to handle it
in case some mild friction
sparks it ablaze and leaves
my scalp black-stubbled
smoking and a stranger.

Inside the skull as well
things have been changing.
Red fingers dip and stir
and raise a froth of brief
intoxication, vibrant,
transforming and a fraud.

A ticket on the concrete,
maimed and trodden, wheels
cool as a white-winged gull
against a bank of cloud.
Under the benches a plastic
beaker bounces, an albino

rabbit, dodging and small,
and quiet elms shake rafts
of leaves in shimmers
of heat or brain tremors.
Our common sight quakes
and diverges and dissolves

into unstable joy.
What we see and what
we know dance merrily
around each other; our furnace
heads, half-crazy with content,
half dread the coming pain.

44

Meeting an Old Man in the Hills

Up here the wind blows cooler than
  it sighed an hour ago.
The town below clicks on at dusk
  its orange-amber glow.
The only track is downward now,
  hesitant, careful, slow,
before the restless calendar
  turns autumn into snow.

Lock

They move that way,
All the few people of the afternoon,
Pulled by the noise of water
Rushing into the lock.
They idle, watching, downwards.

A narrowboat noses the gate.
The water pours. A patient man
Bare feet hushing the deck
Moves in his summer-darkened skin
And watches the slow lift fraction by fraction.

A woman fills the stern
Cradling the tiller across her legs,
Against the heavy child inside her.
The only noise is of water
Roaring in coils as it raises her

Imperceptibly. She with the rudder,
He with a tentative pole,
Balance the boat's position
Inside the filling lock. Ahead
The level there is settling towards them.

Time holds them enclosed as they
Nurture the future. The flow
Will wash this episode out
And drop the next year under them.
The gates creak open like releasing claws.

A Presence

Daily this man stood under the broken
eccentric shade of a palm,
holding his own silence and a mynah
sitting on his shoulder there wheezing,
rasping out its irritated cries.
Edgily everyone listened, as if
trapped in a tangle of metal yells,
as if the other noises in the street
were support for this imposing virtuoso.

At every step he took the bird
cracked open its long bill
close to his ear, and gonged
a high hollow signal to the world.
Not a toe could he lift, nor shift
an arm but the squall of abuse
hit him. It was like the eye
of God watching, relentless, inquisitive,
letting nothing live without scrutiny.

We flowed with the crowds dividing round him
wary or indifferent, wishing
the bird upon him, grateful
for unencumbered shoulders,
for the ears we were taking to safety,
uneasily sensing the squeal
of a coloured bill at the earlobe,
feeling undetachable claws
prickling our own apprehensive shoulders.

Harbour Lights

Out on the flat water
the floating lights preside
over their long reflections.
The hidden ships that ride
at anchor in the river
have swung to face the tide
and all we see from shore
are pin-prick illuminations
on ship side after ship side
where they stand off from harbour.

Stillness imposes itself
from the sky that water
licks invisibly, deck-lights
and stars unquiveringly
mingled and alike. The Gulf
swallows all distance, and lets
darkness after darkness furl away.
What can be seen delights
by imperception, by the deceit
in the whole dark-sparkling mirror.

The world is doubled and
inseparable. Water, sky,
mimic each other's planes
and hang their lights unfixed
to either. The baffled eye
promotes the ambiguity,
its signals undeciphered.
We conjure what it means
inside ourselves, afraid
reflection is reflection and a lie.

Looking Down from the Temple

Smeared air over the city, across
   its almost liquid shimmerings,
under the indigo bowl staining
   to ochre at the edges, holds
off the clearest sunrays; only
   lines of traffic, static or straining
forward in centimetres, angrily
   polish the light.

From here the hard design,
   nude cubes of concrete, ruled
crevasses of streets, reveals
   its logic; like time it drives
unstoppable, dropping red-tiled
   pin-head domes of churches under
the feet of office-blocks, disdained
   into shadow.

This temple broods above all of it.
   High, out-massing the blundering
accompaniments the century
   has flung round, she has always
sky behind her, open and uncontrolled,
   endless and indeterminate.
And even there come the straight-edged contrails,
   creeping, creeping.

Crossings

The riverbed mud
for hundreds of yards
crazed into dried lozenges
crumbles at every tread.

A network of cracks
covers everything up to the centre
where a hint of wet
struggles to seep through
and greases it smooth.

At a fording-place
big wheel ruts trench
across; between them
deep leg-holes where slow buffalo
lurched before the weight
of a sticking cart.

From beyond tall grasses
blowing between riverbank
and distance, the gentle howl
and rattle of an Indian
bagpipe band pushes firmly nearer.

Their white gaiters chalk
the drum-beats; their kilts
swing uniformly under the trail
of wild alien music from cold hills.
On hot tarmac the clack
of boot heels carries them on,
a quirk of history. They march
at right angles to the world,
march, march, the past in their cockades.

The wheel tracks are filling
slowly as the water rises.
When later in this month
the rains drive the river through
here, deafeningly, when it churns

over the ford and even slithers
outwards onto the road, then
nothing will counter it.

The current will carry everything
headlong. There will be no trace
of the ford, no crossings anywhere,
no awkward angles holding up history.
Its pitching force will have
no opposites, no rivals, no survivors.

On the Shore

The small high shrieks of stones
ground one on another,
the disturbed grunts of them,
the doubtful rumble
give way towards the water
to the regular sliding clump
and hiss of feet on minor shingle.

A hundred yards of roller falls
with a belly-shaking detonation
and swirls in the ear and eye
a quarter-minute's chaos of collapse.
The next swings over its own roar
and bombards the escaping slither.

This place is a language, full
of noise and trickeries, the clash
of gravelly phonemes, the uncertain
footing, the long incalculable
rhythms. Here is the grip of senses,
the rich and touchable illusion.
Lick your lips and you can taste salt.

Landlocked

My friend the Hungarian poet
lamented the loss of the sea
that border changes brought,
in war, in history,
decades before she was born.
As a nation we are torn,
she said, out of our past
like a difficult birth, and move
noses up, sniffing for sea-mist,
alert in every nerve.

Beyond the Danube Bend
an ocean of grass is rolling
under an easterly wind.
The mileage of dusty maize
and sunflower fields is swelling,
falling, season by season;
and westward, Balaton,
the largest lake in Europe,
three modest metres deep,
covers its shame in haze.

Always there is this itchy
reaching for something other,
the chafing heads of grasses
restlessly mimicking water,
the wind-stirred tetchy
lake impeding its ferries.
Always the wish to be ocean:
unmarked, indefinite, changing,
a further and further horizon
opening, offering, promising.

House Wall

Here lichen colonises
every domestic stone.
When the eye moves in
close, these millimetres
of territory invest
themselves with light.

The grey wall bristles
rough, shadowed, many-coloured,
each particle an escarpment,
a ridge, a roll of landscape.
Fissures of rivers divide
states, and become defendable.

There are sites for cities, regions
to grow cultures, routes for trade,
airspace to be monitored. The spread
globe squeezes in here, dinning
its inescapable echoes,
mocking and dismaying.

The Wasp Trap

Yellowtail wasps keep coming to the jar,
coming all afternoon.
They hang in the air, dither and pass,
then aim at the hole in the lid.

Someone is trying to be rid
of a seasonful, or to clear an acre,
and could well win. The smear
of honey, sweet gold on the glass,
is packing them in.

The whole engine buzzes energy:
the wasps click into the tacky space
they are machined for;
low over the ground they waver
following the tendrils of scent
neatly to their exacted end.

All hours allow them to enter,
to duck deep under into the sunlit
swollen noise of the hollow tomb.
They cluster and vibrate, then singly
close their systems down.

The dropping sun will put a red
blaze in the glass, over the last moist
stirrings; completing for them a pyre,
a salute, a ceremonious
random farewell from the universe.

Stray

I see you mostly through glass
sinuous along the tops of fences
or coiled compact on that tarpaulin roof-slope
eyes undauntedly on mine.

You slide like black oil out of sunlight
over the edge of dark, to move
within your own strange commonwealth
of stealth and brawls and deaths and frenzied couplings.

I hear you from my sleep and disown
everything. You are not mine.
Only your prints in the damp soil
acknowledge you on my territory,

wilful hedonist, entrapped in no
controlling net of circumstance.
You ink across the new white morning
yawning pinkly with little teeth.

I sit on the wall which divides us. You
prowl rub-rumblingly around my legs,
as if innocent, and I, as if innocent,
look softly on you and absorb the dark.

Windfalls

Apricots, green and unripe, are piled
basin by basin on the windowsill.
Sunwarmed they have the feel
of the barely bloodstained gold
the wind has kept them from,
though their tight skins hold no gradual
dawning pallor to mellow them,
nothing to guarantee what the hands tell.

They are acid-packed, these honeytalc
aborted blocks of summer. Our knowing palms,
practised in surfaces, are here misled
by old anticipation, as the eye instead
insists on Now, shut to the flush that warms
in the implication of that touch of silk.

Still Life

Consider the solidity
of a pear,
            tear-drop
in bulbous amber
gravity-downdrawn
stretched from its stalk
weight hanging
                down out
of clusters of leaves
flower-end star measuring the dive
to ground.

            Take note
of the taut skin-stretch
the about-to-break-out white
pushing behind it
                the sweet
wait for time or wind to bring
the severance
                the drop.

It is all a vast expectancy,
promise, hope,
                fear.

Well-Heads

I

The camel pads and pads to follow
a circle enclosing a well.
The coupled horizontal pole
creaks round, and the jugs lift
over, tip out their silver waterfalls
and dive again into the narrow
darkness of the well-shaft.

The sand is hardly marked
by decades of treading. The last
thousand of the years these wells
have splashed and squeaked
in a daily sun-hammered quest
are a snippet of their time; the miles
of camel-track coil back intact.

II

In other climates
waist-high round walls mark out
a green dark where the buckets
drop to a splash, hollow and distant;
manhandled upwards they glint
with cold light,
jewelled behind the parapets.

These places centred once
the speech of parishes. They hung
on their flat-topped stones,
in the cold morning, the slow evening,
encounters, gatherings of chatter,
round the windlass groaning
over and over at the lift of water.

III

Sometimes a hedge-bank leans
over a glassy block of liquid
held at a slow tremble

down among bundles of ferns
or set in a blackberry tangle,
brim-full and squared
by flat green stones.

So clear as to be nearly
not there, the water touched
has the shock of ice,
breaking shards of brightness
out of the deepest hollow
dark. Purity clutched
from a ditch. The eternal surprise.

IV

They are all, of a kind,
shrines. Carved with the titles
of saints, or decked in any case
with wreaths at festivals,
or round and tensioned
like hubs, each of them signals
a way to the gleam in the darkness.

They all reach down to something
other than water; they find
a way to the vital, waiting
above the fissured ground,
above the inaccessible, intent
on the slow flow of meaning,
the resolving, glittering astonishment.

Marching to Breakfast

We marched to breakfast that winter
   as the sky grew streakily pale
and the frostglaze made boots skid
   and the corporal's wild Welsh tenor
sang out by the cookhouse his long Right Wheel.

Hundreds of feet above us tracked
   echelons of white-fronted geese
their precision visible against the blank
   sky between clouds. As we locked
our feet into the step and banged across

the tarmac glittering with cold
   the geese were fixed in flickering endless
lines, right from the tousled marshes of the Dee
   towards our breakfast and beyond,
making for somewhere else with amazing purpose.

Above the rhythm of our pace
   we still could hear the deep
staccato of their station-keeping cries.
   Each dawn since then has been both gain and loss:
we walk unfettered but with doubtful step.

Walking on Frogs

They get so thick on the ground
    you can't help
walking on them; at every step
    there's a snap
and a feel of giving. These frogs,
    child's eye size
or smaller, baby's thumbnails,
    black in the dusk,
spatter across the road in hundreds,
    feeling their landlegs.

Climbing the road we dodder
    like drunks on stairs
reluctant to trust another foot
    but shoved by weight
to land it somewhere. Frogs die
    in ones and pairs
and multiples and keep on coming.
    They flick across
wet tarmac from the dripping grass
    to a flat finish.

On then, knowing no other way,
    a risk a yard,
and even our small collisions,
    elbows, shoulders,
unbalance and betray us.
    We move confused,
conjoined in indecisions,
    and envy those
thick boots that come down hard
    and walk direct.

All the Small Adventures

Turning your lire, drachmae, dollars
   into fruit, souvlaki or boysenberry ice
you are as nimble-fingered as you are quick
   in reckoning
              and you turning
competently back to the street
   shaded by an enormous mountain
or by the spiderwork of a suspension bridge
   losing itself in mist
or backed by uncountable miles of dead territory
   are never diminished by scale.

Diving into the metro to be whistled
   under the Danube to the Ministry
offices in Pest
   rocketing in an elevator
to the top of the tallest building in the world
   balancing in the stern of a metal pirogue
to thread the alligator waters in the dark
   of a tangled overhang of vegetation
you manage
            a nonchalance
in the face of the world's eccentricities.

Climbing into a locked-up pre-Minoan
   burial ground on an empty hillside
chorusing Hamlet's soliloquy with two
   black brothers and their white
ex-schoolfriend, scholars all,
   at the absolute
apex of the St Louis arch
   listening to the Palestinians from Jordan
explaining their biographies
   you smile with all the living
              and all the dead.

Walking towards me in the reddened
   dramatic air of sundowns

you accept a richness of colour
   from the opposing light
reflecting
            celebrating
   whatever collides with your presence
whichever bit of the world is there
   to be encountered
                  entered
                        and defined.